THE CHECKLIST MANIFEST MUSIC WEBSITE:

ANSWER THIS 9 QUESTION WHEN CONSIDER TO BUILD YOUR WEBSITE

2024

ANSWER THIS 9 QUESTIO TO BUILD YOUR WEBSITE

The hardest part of building a website for your music is getting started.

Here are 9 things to consider when getting ready to build your band's website:

- Brand Name ___________________
- Brad Photos ___________________
- Brad Bio: ___________________
  ____

- Create a custom email address
  ____

- Prepare your music
- Choose a web host
- Choose your website template
- Select your domain name
  ____

- Build your site

Choose an original band name

☐ **Choose a name you can grow and evolve with over time.**

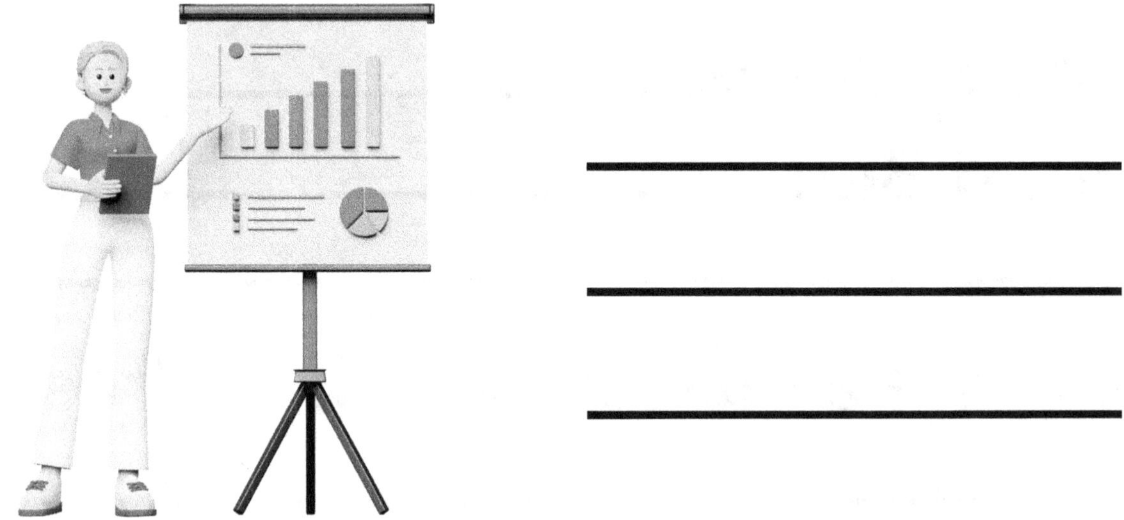

____

____

____

☐ **Make sure the name is not already being used.**

☐Check what the name competition is like online. Choose a name that's unique and easy to search online (not already a popular name/term).

☐ Consider customizing your name with;

- alternate spellings (ex. "Alvvays"),
- unique punctuations (ex. "Therapy?"),
- abbreviations (ex. "Peter Cat Recording Co."),
- unique characters (ex. "AC/DC"),
- use of a statement (ex. "Panic! At The Disco").

Prepare your band photos

☐ Capture high-quality images.

☐ Make sure they represent your band's tone, style, and message.

☐ Take plenty of extra images to have available for press, social media, and promo.

☐ For a website you'll need at least one image that is:
- landscape format,
- 1500 x 1200 pixels,
- center-focused positioning with space on all sides (so it looks nice on desktop and mobile).
- Get creative! It's your project; there are no rules, and no competition. Explore your ideas and create something unique.

FREE MERCH FOR PREMIERE DJS

Voted best emerging music exposure tool.

Every decade or so something special comes along and shakes up the entire music industry. Spinstatz is that one thing that can change the entire music industry as we know it!

Write your band bio

☐ **Include details on:**
- how your band started,

___

- what your band is (i.e. a classic rock trio),

___

- where your band is from,

___

- where your band is currently located,

___

- the band's musical style and genre:

  ____

- any accolades, nominations, and achievements received by the band or its members:

  ____

- any notable tour or show history:

  ____

- all past and upcoming releases:

  ____

- any ongoing projects and collaborations:

  ____

Create a custom band email address

☐ Make it easy to remember.

☐ Keep the spelling clear to avoid typos.

☐ Choose an address that reflects the band name.

Prepare your music

☐ **Use one of these audio formats:**

- **16bit/44.1khz,**
- **24bit/48khz WAV,**
- **320kbps MP3.**
- **Ensure that your tracks have good sound quality.**

☐ **Include cover artwork that's at least 1000x1000 pixels in size.**

Choose a web host

☐ **Verify the following with your web host:**

- storage and data transfer limits,
- the audio files they support,
- their website uptime,
- loading speed from their servers,
- the ease of use of their platform,
- the quality of their customer support.

Choose a website template

- [ ] **Look for features and layouts designed specifically for musicians.**
- [ ] **Does the template use a responsive layout that adapts to different screen sizes and mobile devices?**
- [ ] **Can the website be customized without needing to use coding?**
- [ ] **Is it easy to edit your website?**
- [ ] **Do you have options to switch templates?**
- [ ] **Is there an additional cost to use different templates?**
- [ ] **Does the template support audio and video?**

How To Use Spinstatz

A Record Pool That Pays DJs

★★★★★

" We just couldn't believe there was actually a company that is paying DJs to play music. We thought it was a scam."

LETS'S GO TO PUBLIC
CENTRAL CONNECTIONS

M
MICHEZ
Let's Go to public

Select your domain name

☐ Include your band name in the domain (i.e. yourbandname.com).

☐ Verify the domain registration cost and renewal fees.

☐ Establish your domain extension (i.e. .com, .net, .ca, depending on what is available to register).

☐ Evaluate alternate domain options (ex. if "daisyjones.com" is not available, try "diasyjonesmusic.com" or "iamdaisyjones.com" or some other close variations).

Build your website

☐ **Use a website builder that provides:**

- templates designed for musicians,
- easy code-free editing tools,
- reliable music players,
- SEO for musicians,
- web hosting and domain name registration,
- robust fan data and analytics,
- specialized music promotion tools,
- built-in mailing list tools,
- integrated music services,
- musician-friendly support.

☐ **Sell music, merch, and tickets directly through your website.**

This checklist helps you dive deep into each aspect of your website to make sure you're ready to go live. Check off the items to ensure that you've got everything you need to make the most of your band's website.

Once that's set up, check out <u>How to make a music website</u> if you'd like to go through each aspect of your website in more detail.
Make a mobile-ready music website in just a few clicks.

You can create a unique and modern business website for musicians for FREE

<u>Build your website with Bandzoogle today!</u>

DJ MICHEZ

TOTAL SPINS: 468

Country: Yugoslavia

State: Serbia

City: Serbia

Venue: Empty

SOCIAL MEDIA

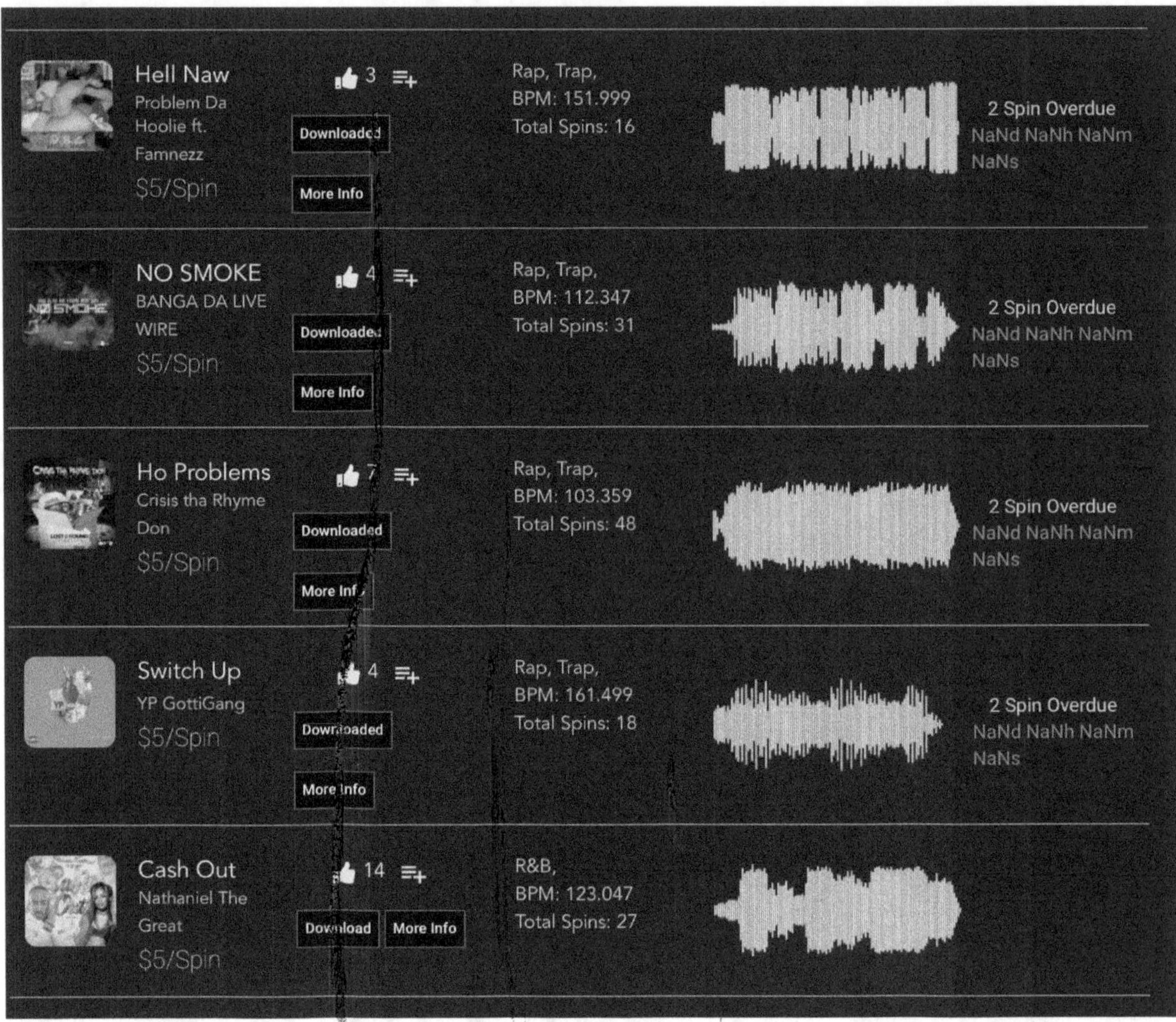

Hell Naw
Problem Da Hoolie ft. Famnezz
$5/Spin
3
Downloaded
More Info
Rap, Trap,
BPM: 151.999
Total Spins: 16
2 Spin Overdue
NaNd NaNh NaNm NaNs

NO SMOKE
BANGA DA LIVE WIRE
$5/Spin
4
Downloaded
More Info
Rap, Trap,
BPM: 112.347
Total Spins: 31
2 Spin Overdue
NaNd NaNh NaNm NaNs

Ho Problems
Crisis tha Rhyme Don
$5/Spin
7
Downloaded
More Info
Rap, Trap,
BPM: 103.359
Total Spins: 48
2 Spin Overdue
NaNd NaNh NaNm NaNs

Switch Up
YP GottiGang
$5/Spin
4
Downloaded
More Info
Rap, Trap,
BPM: 161.499
Total Spins: 18
2 Spin Overdue
NaNd NaNh NaNm NaNs

Cash Out
Nathaniel The Great
$5/Spin
14
Download   More Info
R&B,
BPM: 123.047
Total Spins: 27